E

An Introduction to Emotional Intelligence for a Better You!

Joan M. MacMillan

About the Author

While actively working through her own mental health ups and downs, Joan gained some valuable insights into what it really means to be happy and well. By becoming more curious about views that were different from her own, engaging in new learning opportunities, and practicing continuous self-reflection, Joan was able to make key connections between a variety of new information and experiences leading her toward a more balanced and enjoyable life. This adventure into self-discovery was so powerful that it inspired the departure of her college teaching position to embark on a new, albeit nerve racking, path.

Joan's current path focuses on sharing the kind of knowledge, perspective, and understanding that can offer a deep appreciation of what it means to live a meaningful life in today's complex world. Having completed post-secondary schooling in physical education, athletic therapy, and sport psychology, and currently working toward achievement of her Ph.D. in Developmental Psychology, Joan is able approach the topics of humanity, health and well-being, and emotional intelligence through a holistic lens converging in physical, mental, and universal wellness.

While founded on evidence-based research and current psychological theories, Joan's writing speaks to readers in a personal and profound way. Her own humanity spreads through her words and stories creating a sense that she's invited you in for a friendly chat. Joan is a writer, researcher, and educator - but it's her ability to help people feel seen and heard that will keep you connected long after you finish reading.

Table of Contents

Chapter 1: Introduction to Emotional Intelligence 1

Chapter 2: Why EQ Matters 4

Chapter 3: Where Did All the EQ Go? 8

Chapter 4: How to Move Forward Fruitfully................................. 15

Chapter 5: Clueing It Up... 20

Appendix A: Mindfulness Activity 24

Chapter 1

Introduction to Emotional Intelligence

Have you ever found yourself wondering how we made our way to this chaotic place whereby it seems that to find someone suffering from mental health issues, you only need to open your eyes and look forward? Remember when it used to be people in their 70s and 80s who would speak to 'the good old days, when things were simpler' while now you can hear the same tune being sung by someone in their 30s or 40s? We now live in a world where 1 out of every 2 people in the United States and Canada will have experienced a mental health disorder by the age of 40.

How are we enduring a time where children between the ages of 6 and 14 are dying by suicide at unprecedented rates, before they even know what it means to really live? I'll tell you how – because we are living in an increasingly technologically driven world, and we haven't yet come to terms with how it is impacting humanity. More specific to our topic, we haven't made the necessary connections between the mental health implications in our current way of life, through the lens of emotional intelligence.

Human development is founded on the need for social interaction and belonging, trying and making mistakes, and depending on our ability to feel, think, process, and analyze so we can learn from our mistakes toward continued prosperity. We are shaped by the support and feedback we receive from those within our social clans. This growth, development, and learning on which we depend for our survival and ability to thrive, starts the moment we are conceived. To be well, we need some semblance of health. Yet to be healthy, we must find ourselves well. It's a bit of a conundrum, certainly. However, one that can be massaged and shaped by each of us into a dynamic continuum of health and well-being, if we so choose. We currently find ourselves struggling, as a species, because we are now sharing our homes, our minds, and our daily lives with technology and doing so has circumvented our opportunity for exposure to one of the fundamental things that make us human. Interpersonal connection.

We spend less time in physical contact with people, we are exposed to fewer social situations as we grow, we conduct much of our social interaction through technological means, and we are highly driven by a societal pressure of perfection which is an unattainable objective. Technology has changed the way we relate to one another, which has inherently altered the way we grow and develop as humans. To be more direct, it has impacted our ability to learn and develop executive functioning skills related to emotional intelligence, which form the cornerstone of mental health and wellbeing.

Often termed EI or EQ, emotional intelligence can be explained as our ability to be aware of our underlying emotions, combined with the capacity to process and respond to them in a manner that is productive and healthy for ourselves and those around us. It also encompasses our ability to perceive and respond to the emotions of others in that same way.

Emotional intelligence is a term that was coined in the 1960s by Michael Beldoch, and about thirty years after its inception, researchers Salovey and Mayer expanded on the concept by creating the first model of emotional intelligence. Since then, EQ research and understanding has come a long way leading to the development of additional frameworks. Each focusing on emotions as a catalyst to human behavior while viewing this complex mind-brain relationship through varying lenses. My views of emotional intelligence have been influenced primarily by the mixed model framework proposed by Daniel Goleman in his 1995 book titled, 'Emotional Intelligence: Why It Can Matter More Than IQ.'

EQ involves a combination of self-awareness, emotion regulation, empathy, motivation, and social awareness. Devoid of these skills, we find ourselves unable to relate to, belong with, or learn from, other beings. EQ matters because without it, we often find ourselves feeling isolated, lonely, and unable to resile through the many hardships life has to offer. Without EQ, it can be difficult to find a sense of health and well-being among the constant realities that draw us away from social connectedness and toward an existence overwrought with loneliness, struggle, inequity, loss, and the many other adversities that go hand-in-hand with life.

Having EQ allows us to engage with ourselves and others in authentic ways that promote self-discovery, understanding, and an open mind. A high level of EQ positions us to contribute to the health and well-being of anyone with whom we interact. Why? Well, it's because emotions underpin everything we do as social creatures.

Through generations of evolution, advancement, and change, a certain clarity remains that as a human species, we cannot thrive in isolation. Our biological and psychological makeup is inextricably entangled with an inborn need for social interaction, love, support, and belonging. Yet we have spent the most part of the past half-century navigating a new reality that fundamentally removes us from that which makes us human.

Like other evolved species on our planet, we humans are driven by our innate emotions. However, unlike other species, humans have a capacity for higher-level thought, processing, and analysis that permits for intentional decision-making. Our capacity to make conscious decisions is what allows us to thrive as a species. If we want to do more than simply endure our limited yet wonderous time here on Earth, EQ matters.

Chapter 2

Why EQ Matters

Emotions are the primitive driving force behind our thoughts, decisions, and actions in our everyday lives. While much of 'how' emotions are formed still remains unanswered, due to the progress made within the social sciences over the past century, we now have a much deeper understanding of how emotions are connected to both our involuntary and conscious behaviors. Furthermore, we have gained an understanding of what we can do to help ourselves integrate our emotions into better daily living.

Throughout the 18th century, as scientists and medical authorities of their time began to better understand the human organism, it became common practice to isolate each bodily system from the rest for the sake of deeper learning related to everything each specific system had to offer. Because of this, traditional healing that was previously founded in treating the body, mind, and spirit as a whole, became overshadowed through a century of research and medicine dedicated to fixing or healing the broken part of the whole, as separate entities.

For example, if someone is having pain in their leg it is not uncommon to provide them with anti-inflammatory or pain medication and physiotherapy on their leg. Sometimes this type of treatment works. However, often it does not. One of the main reasons for this is because no matter where our issue is physically located on or within the body, it is the nervous system that functions to sense, manage, and ultimately heal the issue.

Each time we perceive an issue, while the brain and nervous system are doing their thing, the mind is doing its own thing. The brain and the mind, while apparently undistinguishably bonded, are two distinct entities. We can medically treat the body with our new-age medical ideals, technology, and pharmaceuticals, and we can offer psychological therapy to treat issues of the mind. However, we (particularly in the Western world) have moved a long way from the recognition that the best way forward is to treat the mind and body as one unit. What we are quickly learning (or better yet, relearning), is that if the mind and body are not aligned, the health problem that was causing the issue can continue to be 'felt' and 'perceived' by the mind long after all physical evidence of its existence has been eradicated.

Recent learning and understanding related to the mind-body connection is slowly bringing us back to a renewed acknowledgment that by understanding the full picture and treating the whole being, we can better maintain and regain both physical and mental well-being. This is why EQ matters. Our mind, including those complex and strong emotions that are responsible for all that we are, is a key factor related to overall health and well-being. If we can learn to train our minds toward self-compassion, reflection, mindfulness, and connectedness, we can help ourselves find peace, joy, and purpose despite all the hardship that makes its way into our world.

A person with a clear understanding of who they are - who is able to recognize and regulate their emotions, keep their mind open enough to empathize with the emotions of others, and someone who understands the emotional connections to behavior – well, that person will be able to find a sense of joy and calm in most any situation. Not because they've transcended the rest of us, but because they've simply built the operative mental skills that are necessary to prevent our impulsive and strong emotions from dictating our thoughts, beliefs, actions, and behaviors.

It becomes much easier to find happiness in life when we feel as though we have ownership over our own lot. The longer we focus on the need to control everything and everyone around us, the longer we remain unwell and divided within, and among ourselves. Emotional intelligence helps us acknowledge that we are the only entity within our control. If we put some effort into it, we can live in a manner whereby our emotions stop controlling our reactions, thoughts, beliefs, actions, and, ultimately, our lives. From here, we can choose health and well-being, happiness, and joy, rather than waiting for it to be presented to us based on some believed right or merit.

As previously mentioned, emotional intelligence consists of five overarching areas for skill development, including

1. Self-awareness
2. Emotion regulation
3. Empathy
4. Motivation, and
5. Social awareness

and we don't have to be exceptional in each facet. We must simply maintain a dynamic balance among them as we grow.

Self-awareness provides an unfiltered grounding as to who we are – the good, the bad, and the ugly. It can be further developed into self-acceptance and self-compassion, whereby we come to love all that we are while continuing to recognize where we can better ourselves. Emotion regulation provides us the ability to identify emotions as they arise without feeling a need to stifle or suffocate them. It allows us to feel the emotions without them taking too much from us and to connect them appropriately with a root cause before allowing ourselves to respond to their presence.

Empathy is one of the keys to finding balance and well-being as it forgoes our need to judge another for their situational reactions and/or responses. Empathy allows us to offer the support of humanity to another struggling being with no ulterior motive, criticism, or need to fix them. Motivation is tied to both self-awareness and emotion regulation. Recognition of what motivates us toward belief and action, in addition to what motivates others toward the same, helps us to work within a social context and toward common goals. Finally, social awareness is a large piece of the emotional intelligence puzzle because it enables us to understand human interaction and social norms through a variety of complex and ever-changing lenses created by situational context.

It used to be that we developed the skills of EQ naturally through our thousands upon thousands of social interactions that started in infancy. Today, however, there are so many variables that remove us from human connection that it becomes difficult, if not impossible, to do so. Consider the fast pace of life, diverse and sometimes challenging living and caregiving situations, fear of kidnappings, mass shootings, bullying, and reliance on social media for communication and connection, and it becomes understandable how we've lost the main ingredient of EQ development.

Human interaction. And lots of it.

Without the natural opportunities for continuous and unique experiences of human interaction from a very young age, many of those growing up since the inception of the Internet and digital technology revolution have been left wanting. Wanting for higher-level functioning skills and abilities that can help them find a greater sense of resilience, stability, and health well-being.

Chapter 3

Where Did All the EQ Go?

Emotional intelligence hasn't necessarily disappeared over the past half-century, it just hasn't been developed and/or empowered as frequently or consistently as it was in the past. The reason for this is likely because we weren't consciously aware that we were developing it in the past. We developed EQ because we were constantly placed in situations where we interacted with people, and they responded to our interactions. We took meaning from their responses, and we altered our behaviors for future interactions. This process had occurred thousands of times by the time we reached adolescents and is certainly more complex than what I've described. But simply put, as social and evolving creatures, over time, we learned how to interact in ways that allowed us to feel a sense of belonging and love, meeting our internally driven psychological human needs while also enabling us to be an asset to our social community.

Not everyone got to this place, of course, with some people struggling, for example, to accurately look inward at their own behaviors, perhaps due to some physical or psychological dysfunction or trauma within their system. But overarchingly, most humans found a way to develop the skills they required to function happily and peacefully as a cog in the wheel of society. As civilization and technology advanced, life became more pressing for those in the adult, teacher, caregiver, and mentorship roles which ate away at the time that was necessary to be able to engage in such interactions with the younger humans in their lives.

Parents started spending less time at home, children started schooling at an earlier age, we began stuffing more children into each classroom so teachers had less time to spend bonding with each child, and children started spending much less time at the playground, at their friend's house, and speaking to rando's and strangers. All of this accounting for missed prospects of emotional intelligence skill development, therefore creating generations of humans who are not well equipped to manage life's setbacks, stressors, and disparities.

Attempting to navigate life without the learned and developed skills related to emotional intelligence is akin to jumping into the water without knowing how to swim. It leads to an existence whereby everything we are doing feels as though it's just enough to keep our head above water… until it isn't. At which point, we become fraught with physical and/or mental ailments resulting from an abundance of pent-up stressors and unreleased energy that has been cycling within our minds and bodies without an option for a healthy release.

When we are exposed to stimuli that evoke an emotion within us (for example, by seeing something uncomfortable, or by being ridiculed, or perhaps through the loss of something or someone important to us), our minds and bodies, or in other words, our whole being, involuntarily becomes involved in the reaction and response to the stimulus. When our emotions are evoked (which is an ongoing theme of life, happening all day, every day), how do we go about recognizing those emotions, processing them, and responding to them (or doing none of that and simply reacting by impulse) is highly correlated to our ability to handle and mitigate stress so that it doesn't leave us feeling unwell, exhausted, and searching for air.

If we manage and regulate our emotional responses through a lens of emotional intelligence, all of the biological and psychological implications that result from the involuntary emotional responses remain balanced. And typically speaking, balance in any life system contributes to health and well-being.

Consider the following situation: *You are 13-years old, 25-years old, or 45-years old, and you are having a conversation with a small group of peers. You make a comment or offer a suggestion as* *to how a certain problem can be solved, and your peers begin mocking your idea, laughing at the stupidity of it, and placing an uncomfortable – spotlight – right – on – you.*

Such a scenario would typically evoke a sense of embarrassment, anger, shame, self-judgment, and a myriad of other emotions. And when we are hit by these emotions, if we allow them to direct us, they welcome involuntary changes in our heart rates and breathing rates, increased blood pressure, and altered neurotransmitter and hormone release, to name but a few.

You see, our emotions, if not recognized and regulated, can alter our biological structures and functions in an acute and chronic way. Additionally, as these emotions get bigger and stronger, they can also lead us to think negatively of ourselves, to shut down in future situations where we might have innovative solutions to offer, or to simply believe that we are not enough. Bringing us back once again to the ever-present mind-body connection of health and well-being. In scenarios like the one above, we typically have three options as to how we are going to deal with those pesky emotions, each one making its own mark on our overall ability to thrive.

The first and healthiest option, is to recognize the emotion, identify it with a name, and either own or reject it. The second option, erupting like a volcano spewing blame and shame everywhere, is less healthy than the first but healthier than the third option. The third option is to ignore it all until it eventually comes back to bite us. Each of these emotional management strategies is discussed below in a little more detail.

Recognize, Identify, Own, or Toss… It's a RIOT!

Recognize that you are feeling the way you are feeling and identify the emotions that are causing you to feel the way you do by naming each of them. Going back to our example, while I'm feeling angry at my peers for mocking me, that anger is grounded in the fear that I might be wrong or might not be good enough. Naming that fear of failure allows me to process it. I can then remind myself that I'm confident in my suggestion despite their responses, rather than focusing on the anger and pointing fingers back at them as being the cause of my feelings. Avoid placing blame on those around you for making you feel the way you do and own it internally.

Remember, the only thing we have control over in this world is ourselves, and we are the only ones who can be responsible for our own feelings. Once you've named the emotions that are stirring, figure out their root cause. If your actions are at fault (i.e., you acted in a less than desirable way and are feeling guilty as a result), own it. Acknowledge your mistake, forgive yourself for your humanity, and offer an apology to anyone who was negatively impacted. Then take a moment to consider how you might respond differently in a future situation, and move on. If your actions are not at fault (i.e., your peers from earlier are simply being inconsiderate jerks at your expense), choose not to wear their inappropriate reactions, and toss it.

You get to decide whether you're going to let another person's reactions and responses leave any lasting mark on you. To do so, you accept that you can't control another person (no matter how annoying, mean, rude, or unbearable they are), and move forward without bearing any weight of their behavior.

This process takes practice, of course, as the act of recognizing and identifying emotions must be learned and honed over time. But once you become grounded in the practice, you'll notice that all of those biological and psychological shifts resulting from emotional responses are no longer taking hold. It's a RIOT, because when your body is introduced to stressors that create emotions, YOU get to facilitate the entire situation consciously by taking hold of the reins. You get to guide the stressors through an active process of healthy release, so they're not left swimming within that mind-body connection wreaking havoc for another time.

Erupt with Blame and Shame.

The second way you can deal with your emotions is less healthy for you and those around you, but it is the go-to method for a lot of people, particularly if they've made a mistake leading to the emotions. If we make a mistake that negatively impacts another human, it's healthy to feel guilt. The emotion of guilt helps us to recognize we're not in alignment with our values, and hopefully leads us toward apologizing to the other person. Instead of feeling guilt in such situations, however, many people feel shame which is unhelpful and toxic. Instead of thinking, "I did something selfish or mean" (which is guilt), shame tells us that "I am selfish," or "I am mean." Shame is a lot harder to process and correct because rather than recognizing acted meanly or selfishly - you believe that you are a mean or selfish person.

If you ever feel like you are mean, or you are selfish – that's shame screaming at you, and it's something you need to speak up to. "No. I am neither of these things. I am human, and I made a mistake, I acted meanly, and that's completely okay to make mistakes." Because if you don't stop these powerful shaming thoughts, you will likely end up screaming something else, somewhere else, at someone else. Or in other words, you wind up erupting with blame and shame at some undesirable point after the event that evoked your initial emotional response.

If you often find yourself losing your cool at colleagues, your kids, your partner, your parents, or the random stranger on the bike trail, you're probably not meeting your potential in emotional intelligence. We usually erupt this way when we are left feeling overwhelmed by big emotions and don't have the self-awareness, emotion awareness, and empathy that's necessary to process our emotions in a healthier way, such as in the RIOT method above.

As mentioned earlier, the whole 'biological and psychological shift' that was created in your system when you started having emotions, must in some way find a release. You might be able to keep that energy contained in the short term, but if you don't find a way to let it out, at some point when you're least expecting it, BAM… you find yourself yelling at your kids with an intensity of a woman in labor, over something small and insignificant that really didn't deserve such a reaction. It's not an entirely healthy release, but a release nonetheless, which at least allows the biological changes to shift back.

Unfortunately, you're usually left with a lasting psychological impact resulting from your poor behavior and the recognition of how it impacted those who were struck by your explosion. If continued over long periods of time, the eruption with blame and shame method of emotion management can slink its way into the final and unhealthiest option.

Ignore it Until it Bites Back.

The third thing that can happen as a result of being faced with emotions includes negative physical health impacts. Returning one more time to the biological and psychological shifts that occur when we have emotions, if we don't RIOT and we don't erupt to release the internal energies created through our emotional responses, those altered energies continue cycling until eventually they find their own way out of our system in the form of disease, illness, or disorder. Increased stress levels that are present for a continued period have been tied to higher levels of heart disease, increased risk of cancer, and decreased levels of sleep, among so many other health conditions. If you can't find a way to release the energy shift from the body, it will find its own release within the body and when your energy shift results in lasting internal changes, your health will pay the ultimate price.

This unfortunate position, is where too many of us currently find ourselves. In a world where so many are suffering from some physical or mental health problem, much of which can no doubt be, related to our inability to identify, process, and regulate our emotions leading to chronic stress and eventually, devastating biological and/or psychological failure within the mind-body system. It's a less than desirable reality, but all is not lost.

As ever-evolving, learning, and developing humans, we have the capability to recognize this relatively newly developed limitation that has been placed upon us through world advancements, and we can respond to it in a meaningful way. We can begin educating people on the mind-body connection and on the benefits related to emotional intelligence. And we can start creating purposeful situations for interpersonal interaction that are necessary for the practice and development of EQ skills from a very young age.

Chapter 4

How to Move Forward Fruitfully

To move forward in the most beneficial way, we adapt... and fortunately, as a species, we have demonstrated adapters! While we used to believe that our brains were finished developing at the age of 18 years old, more recent research in the areas of biology, neurology, and psychology have demonstrated that our brains are not actually fully developed until we are closer to age 25.

That said, well into our elderly years, our brains maintain an ability to change, grow, and continue to adapt. The term for this has been coined *Neuroplasticity,* and it's truly a magical kind of revelation that has led to some exceptional therapies and treatments to heal various injuries, illnesses, and diseases that were once determined to be insurmountable. If you're interested in learning more about the neuroplasticity of the brain, the book *The Brain That Changes Itself,* by Dr. Norman Doidge is a pretty stellar place to start.

In the book, Dr. Doidge takes us through various accounts of patients who had experienced issues such as vertigo, stroke, mental disorders, chronic pain, and the like, who experienced improvement and often the cure of their symptoms through the development of new or enhanced neural pathways in the brain. Proving again and again that what we think we know is often limited by what we've yet to learn. It is through such learning that we will continue to adapt and evolve, as a species.

Back to the EQ of it all, I see the development of emotional intelligence as a form of neuroplasticity. Any time we work to learn, practice, and develop new skills, they are honed through a series of malleable changes that occur within the brain. On a very simplified level, here is what happens within the mind-body system when we process new information:

1. A new stimulus is introduced to the system via one of our sensory organs.
    a. Someone tells us that our response to a situation was inappropriate and/or unprofessional (we hear their words, we see their body language).
2. The new information is directed to the brain and mind for processing through an extraordinary sequence of neural pathways, so it can be decided if action is required.
3. The mind and brain work together to process the new input, considering the emotional responses evoked by the input, any past experiences, knowledge, and information that might relate, and any memories we've stored that can help. This all happens at an incredible speed and if we aren't practiced in emotional intelligence and mindfulness most of this processing occurs without our conscious involvement.
4. Once the new information is processed, and a decision is made, resulting in action on our part. Keep in mind, that if we haven't consciously been involved in the processing phase (which happens more than it doesn't), our decision is not likely going to be a great one because it will primarily be based on emotion and not reflection or logic.
    a. That action might be to yell, walk away, shut down, defend ourselves, blame someone else, or something similar, but that's the end of the typical cycle moving from new information to decision and action.

Where most of us require work and adaptation in managing our emotions, is in Step 3, above. Without having developed the skills related to mindfulness (as an example of a necessary EQ skill), our mind and brain will typically run through that entire process on its own and we are simply left as a bystander to our predetermined actions. Without EQ, many of our decisions are made more by the brain, and less by the mind. Maybe we would prefer not to yell and start defending ourselves in response to news that we acted inappropriately and unprofessionally, but because we haven't learned to pause between impulse and action, once the involuntary parts of our brain have decided on action, we act.

But what if we could set our brains up just a little bit differently... you know, change the layout slightly so we have a little more space in the area allowing us some room to pause? That's what the development of EQ skills provides us. If we were to learn about, practice, and develop the skill of mindfulness, we would inherently change what's happening in Step 3 within our brain and mind, offering us a completely different outcome.

Let's say that our current response in the situation offered above is to raise our voices and defend our behavior. We can consider our normal neural pathway to go something like this:

Receive sensory input – Feel uncomfortable emotions that are formed involuntarily through your lower brain and allow them, in addition to our current level of knowledge, experience, and memories in the area, to dictate the response – Impulsively respond to defend ourselves and lay blame elsewhere because it helps us rid the emotions and any ownership of them.

This response may help us to feel better in the short term because we don't have to believe that we are part of the problem. In the long run, however, it's not helping us to build functional relationships, nor is it helpful in promoting forward movement in our lives and/or careers. Our inborn neural pathways are automatic and steered by our reflexive need for survival, but as we grow, we begin to integrate many of these reflexive impulses into our nervous system and build new and improved neural pathways that benefit survival and our ability to thrive.

This integration and ability to manipulate the wiring within our neural pathways comes from our ability to interpret the feedback we are offered as a result of our behavior. For example, maybe someone helps us to understand that our reactions are limiting to us by giving us verbal feedback on our performance, or perhaps we read a book such as this one and a new perspective helps us recognize that we are limiting ourselves, or we may get feedback by engaging in therapy or coaching (which I am a huge fan of and believe everyone should do). Regardless of how we receive the feedback, somehow, it is brought to our attention that we are hindering ourselves based on our current mind and brain wiring. Once we receive the feedback and are ready to acknowledge that maybe we are part of the problem, where do we go from there?

While there isn't just one answer, a great place to start in altering unhealthy behavior is to engage in mindfulness practice, and as such, I've included a quick and dirty mindfulness activity in Appendix A, to get you started.

Each day, you take 2-5 minutes to engage in mindfulness practice, which begins to ignite (literally) new neural connections between the smallest functioning cells (called neurons) within your brain and nervous system. The more you practice mindfulness, the stronger these sparks and connections become, until eventually, the new neural connections that you've generated become the path of least resistance within your brain and nervous system.

Over time, you find yourself in situations where you might have typically reacted to your emotional drivers, but are now able to take an active role in the decision-making cycle that's occurring in your mind and brain. All because you've created a neural pathway that allows for a mental pause between impulse and action. In other words, you've adapted and you've changed that malleable brain matter to create a space for mental pause, overcoming your prior limitation. If you were to engage in mindfulness practice and continued learning about emotional intelligence and emotion regulation, for example, what you would have done within the mind and brain, is this:

Receive sensory input – Feel uncomfortable emotions that are formed involuntarily through your lower brain, mentally pause long enough to keep your conscious upper brain engaged and begin processing the emotion, and combine this with your <u>new</u> knowledge, experience, and memories in the area – thoughtfully respond to either apologize, or engage in conversation as to what you did that was inappropriate/unprofessional so you can seek to better understand yourself, the situation, and the other person.

At first, it's a conscious effort to build new neural pathways and new skills. No different than if you were learning how to do a cross-over in hockey or play a new song on the piano. Over time, however, the practice becomes the path most traveled, and your new mental skill becomes ingrained and habitual. The adapted neural pathway takes priority over the old path which eventually fizzles out completely due to lack of use.

A wonderous thing about the brain, is the 'use it or lose it' feature related to the neural pathways. The ones that you nourish, use, and develop are the ones that will continue to grow. The ones that you ignore get trimmed and repurposed for other mental ventures. As an ever-evolving and conscious being, you get to choose which pathways you reinforce within your mind and brain. Moving forward fruitfully in health and well-being takes an active effort to choose growth and development on a continuous and life-long basis. And while exerting and continued effort might be the harder choice, it's this effort that will ultimately help us to regain our belonging, loving, and purposeful place within ourselves and society. Knowing that we have only a limited time on this Earth, making the choice to engage in continued self-development and growth allows us to spend that time reconnecting to humanity, for the sake of all humanity that follows.

Chapter 5

Clueing It Up

From time to time, we will all find ourselves struggling through this miraculous life because while life can be glorious, joyful, and exciting, we exist as a species due to our evolved capacity to overcome the various challenges, hardships, and obstacles that have been placed in our path since the dawn of species.

Overcoming adversity is a part of humanity, and the continued need for change and adaptation is one of the only certainties in this very uncertain existence. We may not know what uncertainties or new encounters we will find ourselves up against in the future, but we know for certain that they will be there. We provide ourselves greater odds of finding the glory, joy, and excitement through the obstacles and challenges if we arm ourselves with the skills and abilities of emotional intelligence that allow us to corral even the strongest of emotions within us. We've spent too long attempting to subdue and push down our emotions for fear of them being seen as a weakness or a limitation, and in doing so, we have created for ourselves a world enveloped by the inability to cope.

We have established a norm consisting of limited resilience and increased human suffering, and I'm confident to say that it's not pharmaceuticals that will help us rebuild. It's not the newest medical technology or the fastest trending wellness app on TikTok that will challenge the realities of our current mental health struggles. We have spent the past few decades waiting on some answer, resource, or miracle cure for our global health crisis because we have been too preoccupied, and maybe even a little lazy, to recognize that we are the only solution to our struggles.

If you've found yourself feeling a little (or a lot) down and out, exhausted, angry, sad, lost, or lonely, why not give yourself the gift of growth? Take the time to learn more about emotional intelligence and about how it can help you to become that energized, joyous, purposeful, and focused person you know is within you. In doing so, however, remember that knowledge is only one piece of the adaptation puzzle.

Developing any new skill, be it physical or mental, requires consistent effort and energy. When we are referring to skills of EQ, the effort and energy typically comes in the form of conscious reflection, the written word, practicing mindfulness and meditation techniques, talking things through with a trusted person, and expressing yourself in some capacity. While doing the work internally within your mind is better than nothing, it's not usually enough to get those new electrical pathways within the brain firing at the capacity needed to allow them to stick.

Fortunately, if you do decide to engage in EQ learning and development, the 'practical effort' part of it can be done in as little as 10-15 minutes per day to allow for real change in behavior. As with any other form of skill development, the more time and effort you put into it, the quicker you will get results, and the more you will get out of it. Based on research and experience, I'm comfortable to say that if a person engages in effective emotional intelligence skill development, activities, and practice for a minimum of 15-minutes per day, on a daily basis, they can often see behavioral results occurring in as little as a month or so.

These behavioral changes are usually noticeable by others in the person's social circle, and they will often be joined by notable positive health impacts related to reduced stress, increased energy, and an overall sense of well-being. The positive impacts won't last forever, and they will continue to ebb and flow as we continue to experience setbacks and challenges. However, with continued practice of EQ, we will find ourselves able to bounce back into our balanced, healthy, and joyous state faster and with more ease than what was possible prior to expand upon our mental skillset.

There are therapists and personal coaches who can help you develop these skills, and there are also consultants who engage in the Emotional Intelligence Assessment that is geared toward helping a person get a baseline of where they currently are in their EQ skills and abilities. On a personal level, I went through coaching and an EQ assessment process, and I found such value in the experience that I became certified to offer it to my own clients. I also have a fantastic therapist who I see more frequently when I'm struggling, and less frequently when things are in flow.

I also continue to do my own research in the areas of emotional intelligence, developmental psychology, alternate treatment options for mental health struggles, and overall mental health and well-being. I do such things, because engaging in each of these learning and development practices helps me to continually strengthen the neural pathways that lead me toward resilience, happiness, and purpose. I share them here because some of these techniques may work for you to help you find peace, balance, and joy. But if not, there are so many alternatives that you will likely find what works if you keep searching.

Regardless of which route you take toward better understanding your own EQ skills and working to develop them, so long as your learning and practice are founded in evidence-based learnings and thorough research on the topic, you're on the right track toward meaningful personal adaptation and growth. If, on the other hand, you're not currently doing anything to work toward developing your EQ, reading this short eBook is a great first step. So, just make sure you keep taking steps, no matter how small they may seem, to keep moving forward toward the best version of yourself.

As always, please feel free to visit my website at www.cammaclearning.com for additional resources, services, and information related to the never-ending journey of personal development toward health and well-being. If you enjoyed the read, please note that I will be releasing further installments in the EQ & U series, offering a deeper dive into the EQ concepts Self-Awareness, Emotion Regulation, Empathy, Motivation, and Social Awareness. If you'd like to receive notifications when they become available, please visit the website, and join the email list.

Thank you for choosing to read my book and thank you for being an advocate for human health and well-being. I appreciate your support and interest!

I'm here for you, and I am grateful to have you here with me!

Until next time, take care and stay well.

Appendix A

Mindfulness Activity

People often get different images in their minds when they hear a term like mindfulness. I used to picture everyone removing their shoes and socks and sitting cross-legged on the ground to "ohmmm" while they emptied their minds. This image came from my own ignorance and bias, but again, I'm human, and I've since learned from my misjudgments. The term mindfulness has become somewhat of a 'catch all' term in modern Western society to envelope all things related to 'calming or quieting of the mind.' I will continue to use the term mindfulness, as it resonates with me as a method of being attuned to one's own mind, however, please note that what we will actually be working through here is an ability to become accustomed to a conscious commitment of the mind, and proceed with our commitment while becoming mindful of the impulses that will often set out to sabotage us.

What I am going to introduce to you here, is a simple exercise that you can do to promote resistance to the impulsivity that drives most of our daily behavior. It is a daily check-in with the self that focuses on committing to a stated intention and simply following through on that commitment. Why do this? Did you know the modest act of sitting still for 5 minutes without allowing yourself to move or to react to your thoughts... no matter how itchy your nose gets, can help your brain to resist impulsiveness?

Mindfulness doesn't have to be about controlling your every thought or emptying your mind of thoughts (though it can be if you so choose). It can be about making a verbalized intentional decision and committing to it regardless of how hard your instinctual brain tries to talk you out of it. And trust me, your instinctual brain will work to no end to try to make you break your commitment to stillness. The same way it works to convince you to press the snooze button when you've committed to waking early, or to open the pantry door to grab another snack when you've committed to not eating after supper.

When we practice mindfulness, the impact on our nervous system includes the development of new and stronger neural pathways that work to give us the pause we need in our moments of impulse. If you consider what I'm saying, your actions and daily practices can, in fact, alter your biology.

As mentioned earlier, recent neurobiological research shows that you can indeed teach old dogs' new tricks – figuratively speaking, of course! This means that, as once believed, the adult brain does not, in fact, become fixed once it's done developing. Scientific and technological advancements over the past decade have completely changed what we thought we knew about the human brain, which is why, while it may seem hokey to some, we now know that the simple act of practicing mindfulness on a regular basis can offer you the brain development you might need to move from impulsive reaction to intentional action.

And if all it's going to take is a few minutes each day, and you can do it sitting in a chair or laying in your bed, really, what have you got to lose? Your ego doesn't even have to take a hit because you can do it without anyone knowing! On that note, and to set you up on the path to mindfulness success, let's run through a quick 2-minute mindfulness session together.

While you are engaging in your mindfulness practice, you will sit or lay in calm, intentional stillness until the timer runs out. If you are not able to make it the full 2-minutes because you just have to move in some way, don't quit. Simply get comfortable again, recommit to stillness, and start from that point until the time runs out. Maybe try to keep track of how many times this happens or the ways your brain tries to trick you into moving while you are attempting to keep true to your intention, so you can see progress over time.

Mindfulness Practice:

It is recommended to read through the whole practice in its entirety before beginning to ensure you engage successfully.

1. If possible, set a timer for 2 minutes and 10 seconds (to allow for transition time into stillness).
2. Take a moment to either sit or lay comfortably, wherever you are right now.
3. When ready to begin, start your timer, close your eyes, and make an out-loud verbal commitment to yourself that you will not move for two minutes (see Intention of Stillness below).
   a. Note, this might not seem like a big deal, but let me preface this with the fact that movement includes any kind of blinking, speaking, reacting, coughing, throat clearing, tongue moving, itching, finger twitching, or anything else similar. I'm going to guess that even just mentioning these things has already got your brain telling you that you need to do some of them right away… so get them out of your system before you start!
4. Undertake the mindfulness practice without stopping, until your timer sounds. See tips and tricks on the next page, for advice on how to manage impulses and inadvertent movements throughout your practice.

My intention of Stillness: *"I will not move or react, in any way, for the next two minutes."*

Some tips and tricks for success:

- If you notice an impulse (i.e., an itch), don't ignore it. Telling yourself to ignore it gives your impulsive brain power. Simply tell yourself, "My ear is itchy. That's interesting." But do nothing. Or, "My throat feels phlegmy. That's interesting," and again, do nothing to react to the acknowledged thought. This is the equivalent, in emotion regulation, of us recognizing and identifying our emotions before impulsively reacting to them.
- If you find yourself inadvertently moving, adjusting, clearing your throat, or anything similar, immediately remind yourself that you're human, and simply reset yourself in that very moment, and keep going. No need to start over, just refocus on your intention and continue.
  - Don't allow yourself to chastise or judge your inability to remain still. This way, while you are practicing your mindfulness, you are also engaging in the practice of empathy and self-compassion.
- Once you are able to complete 2-minutes of continued stillness a number of times, enhance your practice by increasing your time commitment, altering your position, or challenging yourself with an additional intention. Remember, the purpose of the practice is to make a clear intention out loud and to remain committed to your intention despite your impulsive brain attempting to sabotage you. If you find yourself thinking, "Well that doesn't really count because…" that might be a good indication that you're being taken advantage of by your impulses and ego!
- Once you've become grounded in your mindfulness practice, start taking the practice into your daily life and using it in the real world. For example, perhaps you can state an intention of, "I'm not going to cut anyone off during this meeting, and I will hold my comments until everyone else has stopped speaking."

The options for development of a mental pause are endless and can offer benefits in any life situation.

Remember, the more you practice, the easier it becomes. Eventually, and with enough good practice, the new intentional pathway becomes the path of least resistance, creating the space you were seeking within your mind and brain, to stop acting impulsively and start deciding thoughtfully in emotional or stressful situations.

Good luck with your practice and as always, keep striving to become better today than you were yesterday!

Manufactured by Amazon.ca
Acheson, AB